THE
48-HOUR
RULE

AND OTHER STRATEGIES
FOR CAREER SURVIVAL

THE
48-HOUR
RULE

AND OTHER STRATEGIES
FOR CAREER SURVIVAL

LISA D. MAGNUSON

Dee Dee,
Merry Christmas
and thanks for your
friendship.
Lisa ♡

MC2 Books
Hurst, Texas

Library of Congress Control Number: Available
ISBN: 1-893347-03-6
Copyright © 2002 by Lisa D. Magnuson

MC² Books/ MC² Publishing is a member of the McGrew + McDaniel Group, Inc.

Book Design by MC² Books
Jacket Art by Tamara Grigsby
Inside Art by Talana Gamah

First Printing, February 2002

The authors and publisher have made every effort to ensure the accuracy of the information and examples shown in this book. However, this book is sold without any warranty, expressed or implied. Neither the authors nor the publisher will be liable for any damages caused or alleged to be caused by the information in this book. The opinions expressed in this book are those of the author.

MC² Books are available at special discounts for bulk purchases. Please contact McGrew + McDaniel Group, 860 W. Airport Freeway, Suite 709, Hurst, Texas 76054 or call +1 817 577 8984.
Find us on the web at http://www.mc2books.com/ and http://www.mcgrewmcdaniel.com/

This book is dedicated to my Mom, Joanne S. Janssen, who instilled in her five children the lifelong value of appreciation; to my husband Bruce who won my heart with a thank you note after our first date; and to my girls, Anna and Sara, who I pray will also live their lives with gratitude.

Lisa D. Magnuson

→ Preface

This book is about thriving at work. It delves into the *over the top* skills needed to make a difference throughout your career. Call them professional effectiveness skills or traits to differentiate yourself from the pack, either way these success ingredients will take you where you want to go. This book is designed to give you valuable tips in the areas of career management, attitude, speed and cooperation.

By the end of the book, you'll know how to use the "48- hour rule" to your advantage. You'll be able to identify the six accountability tendencies in the workplace and decide which approach yields the best results. Finally, you'll be able to package your unique skills and accomplishments to promote "Myself, Inc." throughout your career.

If you're interested in enhancing your career effectiveness and 'winning' more often, read on. Learn why basic business etiquette, gratitude and other subtle work habits will determine the winners and losers in today's competitive market.

You'll meet Robert, an information technology professional. Robert has a good track record of success but has experienced some recent career setbacks. He seeks the help of someone he trusts at work, an advisor, who eventually becomes his mentor. The advisor guides Robert through a comprehensive but straightforward assessment, helps Robert develop a game plan and finally introduces Robert to six successful professionals who share their secrets to maintaining a winning edge.

Work today is crazy. It's like a super high-speed roller coaster. The ride is exciting, fast and you have to hold on for dear life through most of the curves. It seems like you're either on the fast track train or waiting in long, endless lines for a chance to ride again. Those in the back of the train are just trying to survive. They spend the ride anticipating (or dreading) all the ups and downs. Those at the front of the train feel a little more in control. They can see the path ahead and can make the appropriate adjustments to enjoy the ride. Professional careers are hard work whether you're thriving or just trying to survive. Why not put yourself at an advantage?

→ Acknowledgements

Writing a book is definitely a team effort. This book is about making a personal difference in your career. Since business etiquette is at the core of the message, I'd be remiss if I didn't show tremendous appreciation for all the friends and family members who helped me along the way. The assistance fell in two categories: emotional support and encouragement and technical aid. (The latter efforts were enormous!)

Heartfelt thanks to Kevin Craine, editor of *Document Processing Technology* magazine and author of the book **Designing A Document Strategy** who challenged me to "find my voice." This was a new experience for me because throughout my career, co-workers have consistently told me to "keep my voice down." Special gratitude to the virtual army that helped edit my material. The core team consisted of Linda Mirch, Kevin Craine, and Joanne Janssen. Also, I'd like to recognize my co-workers (past and present) and friends who reviewed the content over and over and gave me excellent ideas and feedback. (In some cases more than I was prepared for.) This cast of thousands included Anna, Ricki, Craig,

Cary, Carla, Al, Kristi, Ian, Julie and Jody. Special thanks to the contributors of "The Winning Edge" chapter including Barb Pellow, William Seidel Jr., Jay Tyler, Kenneth M. Mirch, Dorinda C. Parker and Tom Kinsman.

Finally, I'd like to thank my supportive husband who motivated me with his loving cynicism, quick wit and high tech virtual consultant perspective.

Lisa D. Magnuson

→ Contents

Sample Forms:

→ Start Here

Meet Robert. Robert's career, like many careers, seems to be moving along in a positive direction. He works hard and has a good grasp of his job. He has some significant accomplishments to show for his efforts. Recently, however, Robert has been passed over for a promotion. And, come to think about it, he hasn't been getting any of the premier projects lately. Robert wonders if his career has stalled.

Robert, like many of us, is not one to let a situation get out of hand. He decides that this is a logical time to take action and find someone who can help.

Robert finds a willing manager who is experienced, successful and open to lending him some assistance.

Robert's new advisor asks a few pointed questions that many of us should ask ourselves.

- Have you taken inventory of your skills and abilities lately?

- Can you describe the 'over the top' traits that will set you apart in your profession?

- Do you have a career plan?

Robert doesn't have to think hard before responding. The answer to all three questions is "No." Robert had focused all his efforts on current job activities and hadn't thought much about his career goals. After all, if you work hard and do a good job, you will get ahead....right?

The advisor points out that the difference between thriving at work versus merely surviving is often quite small. Successful people instinctively do the things that the rest of us have to work at. The skills and traits that differentiate you in your career are sometimes the most obvious yet the most overlooked. Robert is very curious as to what "skills" will help him move forward. Obviously something is misfiring in his career, but what?

A good way to see the path to better performance, his advisor suggests, is to take inventory of current job behavior. A necessary first step in Robert's goal to "measure up."

Robert sits down with his advisor to answer a series of questions that address skills and traits that tend to be career makers or career breakers. The questions are designed to give Robert a clear picture of his current areas of strength and areas that will require additional focus. In order to gain a comprehensive assessment, Robert is also instructed to find two other people who are willing to act as surveyors. (A scary proposition for most of us!) With an eye toward self-inspection, Robert begins reading the opening statement of "Measure Up!"

→ Measure Up!

Professional effectiveness is a difficult thing to nail down. Yet, in the business world, some people are clearly more effective than others. It's the folks that seem to achieve results with ease, rarely fall behind, maintain a positive outlook and have time for the "little extras" who seem to get ahead. How are they different from the rest of us? Where did they learn to differentiate themselves? Did they simply sign up for personal effectiveness instruction? Unfortunately, the differences between those that sustain career success over a long period of time and those who struggle on a daily basis are quite subtle and rarely taught in a classroom.

The **Professional Effectiveness Scale** is a simple, yet comprehensive assessment tool. It includes key areas that are generally recognized as necessary to build and maintain a career advantage. Although many skills are needed to survive in today's marketplace, the "over the top" differentiators include attitude, communication, speed, resourcefulness, cooperation and career management. Combined, these ingredients for success render a powerful recipe for long term achievement and career satisfaction.

How do you "weigh in" on the Professional Effectiveness Scale? If you find this quiz a breeze and can honestly answer "yes" to the majority of these questions, then chances are your professional efforts are paying big dividends. However, keep in mind that careers are dynamic and skill development is an on-going effort. If, on the other hand, you find yourself scratching your head with each question, then you probably have room for improvement.

Take a few minutes to complete this assessment. Answer each of the questions with an affirmative response ("Yes, I consistently do this") or a negative one ("No, I either don't do this or I'm not sure what this is about"). Give yourself a point for every "yes" answer. Sub-total your points at the conclusion of each section. At the end of the survey we'll tally the score. The results may just surprise you.

Professional Effectiveness Scale

Planning

Do you develop plans for all large projects? _____

Do you follow logical steps in your planning process? _____

Are you able to galvanize a team to tackle a project in a clear and effective way? _____

Do you start your plan with a clear understanding of your organizations, clients or stakeholders goals?

Do you have the ability to zero in on and concentrate on the heart of a problem or opportunity?

Can you maintain focus over a long period of time?

Can you visualize the end result after attaining the goal?

Do you allocate time for long-range planning?

Sub-total: _____

Attitude

Do you maintain a positive, can-do attitude?

Do employees, co-workers and clients see you as approachable, flexible and open to suggestions? (How do you know?)

Do you strike a balance between confidence and a humble demeanor?

Do you include words of encouragement (where appropriate) in your daily e-mails and other interactions?

Do you display an attitude of appreciation by sending thank you notes and going out of your way to demonstrate gracious behavior?   _____

Are you fun to work with, maintaining a sense of humor (or at least composure), particularly during stressful times?   _____

Do you set aside time for creative thinking?   _____

Sub-total: _____

Accountability

Do you take complete ownership for your actions and results?   _____

Do you avoid the temptation during a crisis or stressful times to blame others?   _____

Do you take your fair share of the responsibility when deadlines are missed or projects fail?   _____

Do leaders seek you out for important projects because they know they can count on you?   _____

Sub-total: _____

Speed

Do you consistently do what you say you're going to do without additional follow up or reminders from others? _____

Do you employ the "48-hour rule" and follow up on an opportunity or action within 48 hours or before momentum is lost? _____

Do you find yourself setting the pace rather than following the pace the majority of the time? _____

Sub-total: _____

Cooperation

Are you a team player, able to put the goals of the team ahead of your personal priorities? _____

Do you encourage cooperation rather than competition in a team environment? _____

Do you have the ability to identify and garner resources? _____

Do you value diversity? _____

Can you gain consensus and commitment from others? _____

Do the teams you serve on celebrate their accomplishments? _____

Sub-total: _____

Communication

Do you use active listening skills such as
waiting a few seconds before responding,
summarizing what you've heard or asking
clarifying questions to seek a higher level of
understanding?   _____

Do you make time for uninterrupted
conversation with your co-workers about
important matters?   _____

Do you take the time to explain to co-workers
and subordinates how their contributions
impact the success of critical projects?   _____

Are you proficient with various means of
communication methods such as e-mail, voice
mail and meetings and do you use them
effectively?   _____

Can you easily navigate through various
information sources to get what you need?   _____

Do you anticipate information that will be
required by others (i.e., forecasts, budget
projections) and prepare in advance?   _____

Do you return phone calls and e-mails promptly
each day?   _____

Sub-total: _____

Career Management

Do you maintain an up-to-date career portfolio including resume, biography and record of achievements?   _____

Do you know what key accomplishments you will add to your career portfolio at the end of the year?   _____

Do you know what the emerging skills are in your field that will be necessary for success in the future?   _____

Have you taken inventory of your strengths and weaknesses and do you have a plan to build on your strengths and minimize your weaknesses?   _____

Do you make time for professional conferences or retreats and use that time as an opportunity to renew your career enthusiasm?   _____

Do you network by affiliating with people and organizations aligned to your vocational interests?   _____

Do you have a mentor?   _____

Sub-total: _____

A Final Thought

One last critical point: Your professional effectiveness
plan works best on the foundation of a proven track
record and the ability to achieve results in your industry.
It also requires hard work. As Albert Gray points out in
his book, **The Common Denominator of Success,**

> *"The secret of success of every man who has
> ever been successful lies in the fact that he
> formed the habit of doing things that failures
> don't like to do."*

Scores and Interpretation

Give yourself a point for each affirmative response. Add
up your score. A sample tally sheet can be found at the
end of this section for additional analysis.

Sub-total – Planning: _____

Sub-total – Attitude: _____

Sub-total – Accountability: _____

Sub-total – Speed: _____

Sub-total – Cooperation: _____

Sub-total – Communication: _____

Sub-total – Career Management: _____

Total Professional Effectiveness Score:

Score	What It Means
35 +	If you scored 35 points or above, congratulations! You have a comprehensive approach to your career that will produce short-term and long-term results! However, in the spirit of continuous improvement, read on to build on your successful approach.
27 to 35	If you scored between 27 and 35 points, pat yourself on the back. Clearly you are good at what you do and you're probably enjoying the fruits of your labors. Remember that professional effectiveness is a dynamic endeavor and great results today do not necessarily translate into superior results tomorrow.
20 to 27	If you scored between 20 and 27 points, you have some work to do. Take time to prioritize those areas of weakness and work to improve them. You'll reach greater heights in the future by doing so.
-20	If you scored under 20 points it's time to begin working on a personal effectiveness plan. Start by analyzing your results. Which areas have the largest gaps? Which areas, if improved, will yield the biggest return? Are some areas easier to improve than others, giving you an immediate impact?

For those with lots of courage like Robert who want a true snapshot, try this: Have a trusted co-worker, client and your manager complete an assessment for you. This will give you a well-rounded view of your business effectiveness.

Professional Effectiveness Scale
Tally Sheet

Name: Robert C. James

Date: March

Over the top Differentiators	Score	Possible	Gap	Priority
Planning	4	8	4	A
Attitude	6	7	1	
Accountability	1	4	3	A
Speed	2	3	1	
Cooperation	5	6	1	
Communication	5	7	2	A
Career Management	3	7	4	A
Total	**26**	**42**	**16**	

The toolkit tips section is designed to summarize the key concepts from each chapter. The final chapter includes a convenient summary of all the toolkit tips.

 Toolkit Tips:

✏ Taking inventory of your skills and abilities is paramount to gaining insight before moving forward.

✏ It's important to get feedback from more than one source to paint a clear picture of your current skill assets and liabilities.

✏ Sometimes the most obvious career success skills such as speed, accountability and career planning are the most overlooked.

! "To the man who only has a hammer in the toolkit, every problem looks like a nail."
Abraham Maslow

Now that Robert has a clear picture
of his strengths as well as areas for
improvement, a plan of action must be
developed. Planning has never been one
of Robert's strengths. His task is to
develop a career plan. It's best to start
small and keep it simple. Robert's advisor
points out that most successful people
have a career plan. Many people don't
take the time to plan so this is an area to
stand out among your peers. Thoughtful
planning gives you confidence and shows
you can be a leader. Once the planning
process becomes second nature, it can be
used for large and small projects every
day. Robert is somewhat tentative but
the pain of a stagnant career is greater
than the apprehension of creating a game
plan.

→ The Game
Plan

Do today's fire drills detract us from looking at the long view of things? Has thoughtful planning become a lost art? Have the business realities that demand attention today sapped our energies to plan for tomorrow? The answer is an emphatic yes!

Many companies, managers and employees see the value in planning but lack the time to plan until the current situation goes awry. Even basic short-range planning for projects is often cut short. Problem solving and process improvement are often overlooked or delayed until an important client is lost, corporate revenues are down or departmental funding is cut.

Why wait until a crisis to plan for your success? Follow these steps to create a simple plan for your group, department or business. As a result, you will experience the confidence that comes from knowing that you have a well thought out road map.

These steps can be sized to fit any situation: organizational planning, project planning or career

planning. Clearly, the hardest step is to get started.
Resolve to be one of those peak-performing leaders who
have a disciplined focus on those things that leverage
individual and group effectiveness.

Are you thinking this sounds intimidating, painful and
time consuming? Planning is definitely hard work but
well worth the effort. Start slowly and build your plan
over time. Let your initial draft settle before adding too
much detail. Use a format that is comfortable and flexible
for you and your group. Try a fill in the blanks format,
e-mail exchanges or the time tested clean sheet of paper.
Let's get started.

**Analyze your activities, performance and goal
attainment during the past year.** Build your plan on
a foundation of facts. Some people get stuck here and
have a hard time getting past the analysis to the planning.
Look at the relevant information. Ask yourself what
it means and why it's important. Incorporate that
learning into your plan. It's also helpful to look at
your analysis from your boss's perspective. Make sure
your conclusions mirror your department or company's
definition of success.

> **Robert's career plan example:** What
> did you learn from the skill assessment?
> What are your areas of strength? What
> areas need the most work? Review past
> performance reviews. What did your
> managers say about you? Are there
> any trends from year to year? Dig up
> any additional feedback you can find
> such as personality profiles, job results,
> recognition or awards. Make a list of
> important points.

Gain a clear understanding of your organization/ customer/shareholder's goals. It is always important to understand the outside factors of influence before you set your goals. Department plans must be tied to corporate goals in order to be successful. Project teams should incorporate their clients' objectives into their plan.

> **Robert's career plan example:** Are there any outside influences to consider when developing your career goals? Possibly spouse or family considerations?

Determine who should be part of the planning process. Planning is generally a team effort. It is important to take a moment to think about all the people who should be part of your planning process. Involvement in the plan up front almost always ensures enthusiastic buy-in later. Consider all the people who will be affected by your plans; you can always trim the list down later to keep the group manageable.

> **Robert's career plan example:** Mentors, managers and even professional career consultants should all be considered when developing your career plan.

Document detailed personal, financial and business goals. You've analyzed the facts and identified outside targets that may affect your goals. With your team assembled, it's time to set the goals. Your goals should be straightforward, clear and measurable. Prioritize mission critical goals. The number of goals you set depends on the scope of your project, but it's best to keep the number low.

Robert's career plan example: Most successful people have career goals. They can take the form of a specific job or a set of experiences. Some people also include income goals as part of their career plan. Think broadly about what you want to achieve and in what time frame. Goals should be realistic yet stretch your current skills and abilities. Create goal cards that can be reviewed frequently. An example of a goal card can be found at the end of this chapter.

Establish specific and measurable activities that will lead you to your goals. This step involves a lot of work, as extensive research is sometimes required to determine the steps to get you where you want to go. Start by brainstorming. Once you have most of the activities identified, you can then organize and prioritize.

Robert's career plan example: Tap into books on career planning or check the Internet for ideas. Activities for a career plan should include experiences, projects that build skills, jobs or training courses. Be creative with your ideas. If your goal is to have a specific job, your activities might include getting the job description, interviewing several people who already have the job inside and outside your company, or volunteering to assist a person in that job on a special project.

Chart a time line for all activities. Most people are too aggressive in determining a time line and set themselves up for failure. Don't let yourself or your team fall into this trap. Strike a balance between realistic time frames, getting to the end zone and quality efforts.

>**Robert's career plan example:** Most career building activities are in addition to normal job expectations. Be realistic as to how much time these activities will take to complete. Give yourself more than enough time so you don't become discouraged. Remember that career planning is a lifelong endeavor. Rest assured, once you reach your current summit, there will be more mountains to climb.

Identify all resources required. A resource is anything or anyone who can or must help you to achieve goals. Resources can be financial, people, or tools. Most plans can only succeed if the proper resources have been gathered. Consider resources both inside and outside of your organization.

>**Robert's career plan example:** The resources to help with a career plan are endless. In terms of people, I have already mentioned mentors, managers and professional career consultants. Don't forget respected co-workers, the Human Resources group and former teachers and professors. Tools can include books or tapes, training classes, seminars, industry associations, assessments, surveys, and many more.

Many career resources are free, although any financial investments in your career plan will pay big dividends.

Incorporate training into your course of action.
Sometimes to execute a plan, re-tooling is required. It's important to identify any training needs and build those factors into your timeline. Take full advantage of any training offered by your current employer.

> **Robert's career plan example:** On-going education should be part of every career plan. Education can be formal or experiential. Talk to leaders in your industry or read industry periodicals to determine what skills and abilities will be needed for success in the future. Add those skills to your career plan and determine what activities are needed to achieve the learning that will be required. Ask about career training or resources offered by your company.

Pinpoint potential obstacles that may prevent you from attaining your goals. Every plan will encounter roadblocks. Some may be minor yet some can potentially derail your plan. Anticipate obstacles that may prevent you from achieving your objectives. Think about issues that have come up in the past. Consider market conditions, competitive pressures, scarce resources or just plain bad luck. Ask yourself, "What can go wrong?" This negative planning is critical to the success of your plan.

Robert's career plan example: There are several obstacles that block a career plan. The biggest obstacles are usually self-inflicted - lack of commitment, lack of time, lack of discipline. Other obstacles can include competing priorities such as family or changes in your current job. Those who have taken the time to create a career plan, however, have the commitment and discipline to carry it through. The trick is to identify those things that may get in the way of your progress and circumvent them.

Have a contingency plan in mind. Once the obstacles are identified, consider the options. Can the obstacle be eliminated or is a work around required? Most obstacles are not showstoppers if pinpointed early.

Robert's career plan example: Your career plan should be flexible enough to overcome any obstacles. If you have the dedication and commitment to the plan, you'll find a way.

Set aside time each month to review your plans and make necessary adjustments. Plans were not meant to look great and then be put away, never to be seen again. Yet this frequently happens. Check any manager's office for evidence of business plans gathering dust on the shelf. Schedule time on your calendar to review your plan. The frequency depends on the nature of the plan, but all plans should be reviewed at least monthly. Read through the entire plan from time to time, not just the action points. You'll discover new ideas by doing so.

Robert's career plan example: The best way to stay on top of your career plan is to review your progress with an advisor or mentor on a regular basis. This will keep you dedicated to your plan and also give you the opportunity for discussion, feedback and revisions.

Stay flexible. Market conditions are changing at a very fast pace. The best way to keep your plan flexible is to review it often and make adjustments quickly. Try to identify negative trends before they become obstacles to your plan. Conversely, positive trends or opportunities can arise. The fact that you have a plan in place gives you a foundation from which to build in a short period of time.

Robert's career plan example: Opportunities for growth and development present themselves every day. Having a career plan in place will position you to capitalize on those opportunities.

Share your plan with stakeholders, peers, and customers for feedback. Share your plan and results with stakeholders who didn't participate in the planning process. Ask for their feedback. Stay in touch with these people and keep them up to date on your progress. If you're not on track or timelines are slipping, communication with stakeholders is essential. On the other hand, if you've achieved your goals make sure to share your success.

Robert's career plan example:
Communicate your progress and keep
in touch with all the people whom you
identified as resources early in your plan.
These people should become part of your
"network". Send e-mails, personal notes
or articles that may be of interest. You
never know when you may need to
double back for advice or assistance. (By
the way, this takes time and should be
factored into your timeline.)

**Create a visual display of your progress toward your
goals.** It is essential to keep making progress towards
goal achievement visible. Critical resources may be
engaged in multiple projects, therefore it's important to be
diligent and creative in maintaining mind share for your
priorities. Two very different but effective examples of
visual displays include brief progress reports or a simple
diagram charting results.

Robert's career plan example: Regular
meetings with your mentor and frequent
communication with your network of
supporters should be sufficient to keep
your plan moving. Goal cards also keep
your priorities and progress visible.

**Visualize what will occur and how you will feel after
attaining your goals.** It's important to think of your
goals as if you've already achieved them. What will
happen as a result of hitting your target? How will
you feel? What will you tell your friends about your
achievements? If you internalize your goals with an
undoubting belief then your mind will automatically start

"seeing" all the possibilities. It's rather like when you have your heart set on a particular new car. The only model you see on the road is that model.

> **Robert's career plan example:** It's fun and easy to visualize yourself in a different job with a new and interesting set of responsibilities. What will you do each day? What will you accomplish and learn? Who will you work with? How much money will you make? How will you spend or invest that money? The list goes on and on. Even if your career goals don't involve a job change, it's easy to visualize the new projects and accomplishments that await you. The idea is to be end-result oriented.

Celebrate your success! These celebrations are important for many reasons. First, you and your group deserve it. Also, they mark the occasion. When times are tough later, the team will remember the satisfaction and fun associated with goal achievement and will find the energy to carry on.

> **Robert's career plan example:** Stick to your plan and pat yourself on the back for all accomplishments. Go out for a special dinner after completing a difficult training course. Meet your mentor for golf to discuss progress. Career planning should be highly rewarding and fun. Accomplishments will energize you to focus on the next challenge. Maintaining a long-term positive perspective on your career is the key to a fulfilling journey.

Career Action Plan - Sample

Robert C. James – March Update

Short Term Career Goals: (1-2 years)

- NSA certification
- Find an advisor
- Start classes for masters degree
- Lead a high profile team
- Promotion to Director of I.T.

Long Term Career Goals: (3-5 years)

- Finish masters degree
- Get company experience in the financial area to broaden experience base
- Publish articles relevant to information technology and trends
- Hold volunteer board position to broaden network and develop leadership skills

Areas of Strength:

- Strong analytical skills
- Proactive process orientation
- Good verbal and written communication skills
- Well liked by employees and team members
- Good decision making skills
- Resourceful
- Strong customer skills
- Consistent and reliable
- Leadership / teaching skills
- Self directed learner / open to feedback
- Motivated to succeed

Areas of Opportunity:

- Short and long term planning
- Acting with a consistent sense of urgency (speed)
- Maintaining accountability for actions in a group environment
- Career management

Next 12 Month Focus	Action Step
Skills assessment	Complete Professional Effectiveness Scale
Peer assessment	Find two peers to complete assessment
Create a career plan	Go through planning steps
Look into NSA certification	Schedule time to research NSA classes and test times
Volunteer to lead high profile corporate I.T. initiative	Talk with Chief Information Officer
Look into prerequisites for Masters degree	Research the web for all the details
	Look into company educational support
Informational Interview	Schedule informational interview with Director of I.T. at Az-Tech

Note: Action steps should include a combination of building on current strengths and focusing on areas for development.

Resources Needed	Date
none	February
Previous managers, respected co-workers	February
Advisor	March
Ask Ian about his experience	March
Portfolio of previous successful team projects Endorsement of manager	April
none	May
Human Resources Dept.	May
Friend at Az-Tech	04-02

Toolkit Tips:

✎ Planning is as fundamental as hard work or basic job knowledge.

✎ The hardest part of the planning process is getting started and making a habit of staying with your plan.

✎ Practice your planning steps until they become second nature and can be used each day.

✎ Put your plan in writing. Make sure it's measurable. Keep it accessible. Review your plan frequently.

✎ Plan your career or your career may not turn out as planned.

! "Don't confuse activity with achievement."
   John Wooden, UCLA Basketball Coach

We all know that kids say and do the darndest things, however, we expect a little more from the "adults" at work. It seems that the business world has become a veritable magnet for audacious behavior. We're not talking about the small stuff here - like leaving the copier jammed!

The "Say What" section is filled with true-life examples of bad behavior, lack of general awareness (cluelessness) and serious skill deficits. This list is meant to raise your eyebrows a bit and expose the vortex of gratitude, accountability and manners that we encounter every day at work.

Say What?

A project manager is furious and lashes out at team members when a critical client deadline is missed. After all, the project manager distributed a detailed plan with activities and timelines clearly delineated. *Of course, the project manager neglected to engage team members in setting the goals and timelines. He also missed the step of assuring buy-in and verifying that the team had the skills and resources needed to meet the deadline.*

A large corporation holds a training meeting and fails to plan for coffee, soft drinks or water (not to mention food) at any time during the all day session. *People tend to think of their physical needs first (Maslow's Hierarchy of Needs) so most of the participants probably spent the day thinking about food and drink alternatives rather than the training that was being delivered.*

Goal Card - Sample

Robert C. James – March Update

Goals:	Timeframes:
Identify potential advisor	May
NSA certification	July
Start classes for masters degree	Sept.
Lead a high profile team	Oct.
Promotion to Director of I.T.	TBD

Strategies to achieve Goals:

1. Focus on Career Action Plan

2. Expand on current skill set with certifications and formal education.

3. Expand base of experience through challenging work projects

Training or experience required for goal achievement:

NSA Certification program

Distance learning masters program

The opportunity to lead a high profile project team

People that can help me achieve my goals:

Advisor

Current Manager

Professors

Senior Managers at work

Obstacles to overcome:

Finances to fund certification and masters program

Time to study and do well in school while maintaining performance at work

Availability, timing and readiness for Director's position

Maintaining commitment and focus on my career plan

What will happen after I achieve my goals (Celebration):

Golf day after achieving NSA certification

Weekend getaway after completing masters program

Big family party to celebrate new Director of I.T. promotion

Robert now has a career plan. The process took a lot longer than he expected but it was worth it. He wouldn't have been able to get through it without the help and support of his advisor. Robert is starting to appreciate how much work is required to manage a career. Now that Robert has an inventory of strengths and target areas for growth, career goals and a plan, he's ready to take the next steps. "Before the 'over the top' skills can be addressed" the advisor said, "let's talk about your attitude." Robert was a little surprised. The advisor pointed out how important attitude is in getting ahead. Even if someone has all the training and skills required for a job, if they have even the slightest negative outlook, they won't go far. Robert thought about that missed promotion. He decided to build a solid attitude foundation by incorporating gratitude in his attitude.

→ Put Gratitude In Your Attitude

Has common courtesy become the latest casualty of a business world that forces us to do more with less, faster and better than the day before? In a continual struggle to add value, have we forgotten our basic manners? Has gratitude been replaced by endless demands and thankless work?

It seems there has been a slow degradation of common business etiquette over the past decade. A *USA Today* survey asked workers whether they thought the level of professional courtesy in the workplace had increased or decreased in the past five years and 44% thought that manners had decreased. (*USA Today*, August 10, 2001) As a result, a growing number of people feel that their best efforts often go unappreciated.

Perhaps we have become too caught up in our own success to thank those who have helped us become successful. As a young sales manager during the mid-80's, I recall hearing my boss and mentor tell us to "put some gratitude in your attitude." Those words have real relevance today. Without demonstrating appreciation, how can you expect others to meet your high expectations for success? The famous English poet William James said it best, "The deepest principle in human nature is the craving to be appreciated." Unlike many business challenges today, this particular issue has a simple resolution. As we look to the future and contemplate our increasing technology-based society, we need to consider the "human factor" and the universal need for appreciation. Here are some suggestions to help you put some gratitude in your attitude.

✔ Send a simple thank you note for all courtesies including business lunches, training and other special events. It's shocking how infrequently people do this.

✔ Explain to co-workers and subordinates how their contributions impact the success of critical projects and thank them for their help in advance.

✔ Include some words of encouragement in your daily e-mails. You'll be amazed by the immediate and positive responses.

✔ For any accomplishment ask yourself, "Who helped me with this?" and be sure to thank them.

✔ Go out of your way to do something for someone else without an expectation of repayment.

✔ Never display an attitude of entitlement.
(These attitudes should have gone the way of
the manual typewriter.)

✔ Refrain from office gossip as it will minimize
the importance of your actions when it comes
time to show heartfelt appreciation. Gossip
also tends to have a negative impact on your
attitude.

✔ Find a reason each day to compliment
someone on their effort or attitude and
emphasize the positive impact they have on
you and others.

It pays to differentiate yourself in positive ways. There are
many benefits to following these simple suggestions. First,
you will immediately stand out among your peers and
competitors. Second, people prefer to work with those
people who appreciate their efforts. It's likely that your
co-workers will go the extra mile to help you if they
believe that their efforts will be appreciated. Finally,
showing appreciation will make you feel great about
yourself.

The future will surely hold many exciting technical
innovations, but we can also anticipate the growing
importance of human interactions. Will the digital
marketplace of the future include e-manners? If
our plans don't incorporate daily evidence of gracious
behavior then we run the risk of losing key employees,
clients and opportunities for personal promotion. Surely
gratitude and appreciation should be at the core of
teamwork, cooperation, and communication. Forging into
the future may be uncertain and somewhat scary but

practicing good manners and gratitude is simple and pays big dividends.

Robert started to incorporate appreciation into his daily business interactions. The impact was immediate and the results were amazing. Each time he went out of his way to thank someone or show gratitude it seemed to be returned tenfold. Robert also practiced replacing any negative thoughts with more gracious ones. Last week he included words of encouragement in several e-mails and again was stunned by the positive response. It clearly pays to put some gratitude in your attitude.

Toolkit Tips:

✏ Put some gratitude in your attitude.

✏ Attitude is the ultimate form of differentiation.

✏ Practice showing appreciation each day and watch the positive impact that it will have on you and others.

! "The greatest discovery of my generation is that man can alter his life style simply by altering his attitude of mind."

William James

Say What?

A support team is asked to work through a major holiday to keep critical systems up and running. The team responds immediately and positively, and without hesitation covers the shift. During the holiday, problems arise and the team goes to extraordinary measures, including pulling in additional members to ensure success. The team hears later that a second level manager accepted a special award and company wide recognition for superior service for the effort. The team never received a thank you. *Taking "credit" for other people's work is a lost opportunity for showing appreciation and giving recognition, two things that very definitely motivate people to work hard and to go the extra mile. Also, every company needs to retain its best and most dedicated employees; therefore it is critical to seize opportunities to foster a sense of loyalty by offering recognition for a job well done.*

A manager of a small financial services office collects money from the staff for a going away gift to be given to the operations supervisor. The gift is meant to show their gratitude for years of exceptional support and service. Later the staff finds out that the manager didn't contribute any of his own money toward the gift.

Robert has always been responsible; however, true accountability can be a difficult thing to maintain. Recently, Robert has been involved in projects with several team members across the organization. Sometimes it's impossible to gain agreement on direction, let alone next steps. One of these big projects missed a critical deadline and Robert felt more inclined to blame the organization and team members rather than take personal responsibility. In the end, the lack of accountability and blaming caused the team to be replaced with another group. Robert was beginning to understand that accountability counts.

→ Accountability Counts

We've all heard our co-workers or managers say, "That's not my job" or agree to tasks that they really don't plan on completing. Why are some people consistently accountable and others continually dropping the ball? Is it a matter of intention? Is it a lack of ability to follow through? Whatever the reason, those who lack accountability in their day-to-day efforts will quickly fall behind the promotion curve. Accountability is at the core of achievement and daily career satisfaction. What better feeling is there than leaving work each day knowing you've made your commitments and are on track for long term projects?

Think about your co-workers. Do they tend to be consistent with their accountability tendencies? Are levels of accountability a factor in deciding who should be part of important projects? Do you find yourself counting on the same people all the time?

Accountability in the workplace can be broken down into six distinct categories. The Role Model, Opportunist and Lone Wolf tend to be sought out for critical initiatives.

The Juggler, Flake and Finger Pointer display weaker levels of accountability and for that reason are less desirable when something important is on the line. By understanding the profiles, we can make good choices about potential team members or employees.

The Role Model: This is a person who consistently displays personal ownership for his or her actions as well as the outcome of those actions. This person achieves his or her goals on a regular basis with no excuses.

The Juggler: This is a person who intends to follow up or follow through on commitments but periodically drops the ball. They may be easily distracted or simply have too much on their plate. (Juggling too many plates as the case may be.) They're the ones who seem sincerely sorry when details fall through the cracks or results are lacking. However, upon close inspection, these tendencies are actually habits and it's risky to count on these folks.

The Opportunist: This is a person who demonstrates tremendous accountability but only for marquee projects. Lesser initiatives receive spotty attention by these folks. They are sometimes considered empire builders; if the initiative contributes to their personal goals, you can count on them.

The Flake: This is a person who commits to actions and results but rarely has the ability or desire to follow through on them. These people seldom do what they say they're going to do. In short, you can't count on them.

The Lone Wolf: This is a person who is only accountable to those things that capture his or her interest. Like the Opportunist, the Lone Wolf will give full contribution if the project is in his or her interest zone. Analysts and highly technical people tend to fall into this category.

The Finger Pointer: This is a person who seems to be devoid of any commitment and blames others for mistakes and failure to reach goals. They always have an excuse.

Developing ownership within yourself or others can be a daunting task. Most people believe that you either have it or you don't. National commentator, Bill O'Reilly in his popular book, *The O'Reilly Factor, The Good, the Bad, and the Completely Ridiculous in American Life* points out the following:

> *"The first step to gaining respect is pretty difficult: Always do what you say you are going to do. When you say that you are going to call someone back, you have to call that person back. When you promise to deliver a favor or perform a service, you must come through. When you discipline yourself to fulfill every one of your commitments - no matter how insignificant - you will be respected."*

What are the components of accountability? Do people shift from one category to another depending on the project, workloads or other considerations? Is it possible that by analyzing the factors that make up the behavior we can initiate improvement? Let's give it a try.

The Understanding Factor: Accountability starts with a basic understanding of what's expected. From a broader business perspective, expectations are usually clear. Revenues, profits, earnings are all easy to measure. However, the gray area that most of us live in day-to-day is riddled with unclear expectations and lack of understanding. The funny thing about understanding (or lack thereof) is how straightforward it is to clear up. Simply ask. Ask your boss, client or co-worker exactly what's expected. This works every time.

Some people may not ask because they are embarrassed or think that they should already know the answer, not so. There is always value in testing for understanding. It is important to note here that many people (particularly The Flake and The Finger Pointer) don't really want to understand and use their lack of understanding as an excuse later. But for the rest of us, once we understand what's expected we can move on to the next stage of accountability: the belief stage.

The Belief Factor: Believing that something's important is paramount to commitment. Commitments are usually based on values and personal priorities. If you're trying to hold someone accountable for something, you must make sure that they understand what is expected. This is an area for significant miscommunication and disappointment. Because beliefs can be very personal, people may not speak up when they disagree with the direction or the plan of action. The leader of a project may think he or she has consensus when in fact the group has not signed up for the same end result.

The solution? The leader must build the needed buy-in by involving the group in the process along the way. Ask your group to consider the degree to which they believe in the effort at hand. If they're not in agreement, don't move forward. Be prepared to deselect team members if necessary. It's better to be up front with what can and can't be done rather than let co-workers or clients down later.

The Ability Factor: The ability factor simply has to do with your ability to get the job done. Do you have the skills, experience and tools needed to complete the task? Another pitfall in this area is time. How many times have you over committed or underestimated the time required to complete a project?

There are clearly instances when your "plate" is more full than others. The trick to success in this area is to accurately assess the situation and be accountable only for what you know you can deliver. Learn to prioritize and communicate with everyone that might be depending on you. Better to under commit and over deliver.

The Follow Through Factor: The last major factor is the follow-through factor. This is your ability to close the loop. Some people do great work and forget the smallest final detail. In the end they didn't really finish the job.

Follow through always involves communication and acknowledgement or confirmation that the action has indeed been completed. Ask your customer, co-worker, are we finished? Did we meet your expectations? Were you satisfied with the end result?

There are many useful tools available to help in this area, from elaborate project plans to simple action item sheets. For the mundane accountabilities, action items must be agreed to, documented and communicated if you want to ensure follow up. Use a simple form that identifies: the action that needs to be taken, who's going to do it, the target completion date, and final completion date. This will allow the group to keep track of their progress and will eliminate confusion. Without documented actions, nothing will move forward. A sample accountability counts form can be found at the end of this section.

Accountability Counts

Project: e-commerce initiative

Date of Meeting: 4-15

Date of Next Meeting: 4-29

Action Item	Person Responsible	Targeted Completion Date	Actual Completion Date	Comments
Schedule senior I.S. team to attend next meeting to share company vision for e-commerce	Robert	4-18	4-18	Linda and Dean will share the three-year plan at the next meeting
Identify and evaluate the top e-commerce sites	Dwight	4-22		
Nail down budget for e-commerce project	Robert	4-19	4-19	The CFO (Jody) will outline the budget at the next meeting

Let's look at a few situations and analyze our options. As you read through the scenarios put yourself in the place of the person that has to take action. What would you do? Have you ever been in a similar situation? Can you identify the accountability tendencies?

Situation: You are a sales person with a large computer company. A client has requested a proposal for a complicated solution to be installed throughout their company. The customer reviews competitive proposals and over a period of months negotiates terms and pricing. As you are preparing the final agreement, you notice a large error in the pricing. The error is too significant to absorb and the customer will have to be told. What should you do?

> **Option A:** Tell the customer that the finance department made the mistake and there is nothing that can be done.

> **Option B:** Tell the customer that you made the error and seek a reasonable solution.

> **Option C:** Try to turn the situation around and make it the customer's fault. (i.e., Point out that it took so long to negotiate the terms that the pricing had changed in the interim.)

Do you see evidence of the Role Model and Finger Pointer in this example?

Situation: You are an information technology manager with a group responsible for help desk operations. You are given targets for response time to customers. You don't agree with the goals and feel that they are unreasonable based on the available resources. However, you have an annual bonus tied to achieving the given response time targets. What should you do?

Option A: Get angry with the company for setting unreasonable targets.

Option B: Get your group together and develop a plan to achieve the targets based on the resources that are available.

Option C: Tell your team to do the best job they can and whatever happens happens.

Do you see evidence of the Finger Pointer, the Opportunist and the Flake in this example?

Situation: You are an Executive Director of a volunteer board. You have responsibility to build a strategic plan with very few resources to help. You really need the assistance of the board members to finish the plan. However, all of the board members have full time jobs and other priorities. What do you do?

Option A: Start by doing all the work yourself hoping that if you lead by example the board will recognize your efforts and offer to help. You're making some progress, but many details are slipping with so much responsibility on your plate.

Option B: Seek out board members with specific expertise and try to capture their interest in the project.

Option C: Engage the board immediately in the planning process. Let them make decisions, agree on activities and timelines. Facilitate meetings in which the board members can commit to manageable tasks. Recognize progress immediately.

Do you see evidence of the Juggler and the Lone Wolf in this example?

How did you do? Did your choice of direction seem obvious? Could you identify the accountability tendencies? Sometimes when all the options are listed in black and white the path seems clear. However, these scenarios and others exist in organizations every day. Depending on the person and the surrounding situation, any one of the three options could be chosen. As you would expect, the results will vary greatly depending on the choice.

If you want to be a role model for accountability then you simply have to understand what's being asked, ensure you believe in the goal, garner the resources to accomplish the task and follow through to the end. The business environment values people that are accountable. Even among the most successful CEO's, accountability for results buys points with Wall Street. Those who blame the market, competitors or other factors for disappointing results lose the confidence of the investment community. In the end, accountability counts!

 **Toolkit Tips:**

✆ Are you a Role Model, Juggler, Opportunist, Flake, Lone Wolf or Finger Pointer at work?

✆ Have you considered the components of accountability: The understanding factor, the belief factor, the ability factor and the follow through factor?

✆ Don't underestimate the power of accountability, it is a subtle yet highly valued virtue in the business world.

! "I can give you a six-word formula for success: Think things through -- then follow through."
　　　　　　　　　　　Captain Edward V. Rickenbacker

Say What?

A project team meets for the third time and one member hasn't met any of the agreed upon commitments thereby halting progress for the entire team. *The team is frustrated by this member's lack of accountability but doesn't know how to communicate their irritation without alienating the team member. The team leader or a strong team member must take the offender aside and let him or her know what impact their lack of accountability is having on the team.*

You squeeze in a thirty minute meeting with an associate who needs your help and they show up twenty minutes late, yet still expect thirty minutes of your time.

A director sets up a conference call, which includes over twenty people scattered throughout the country to discuss an important matter. The director neglects to call in, leaving all the participants on hold, wondering what happened. Hours later the director sends an e-mail stating that the call will have to be rescheduled. No explanation or apology is offered. *The director must not realize that his lack of professional effectiveness (and general awareness of manners) in this situation will translate into lack of commitment from the group later. In accountability terms, this director is a Flake.*

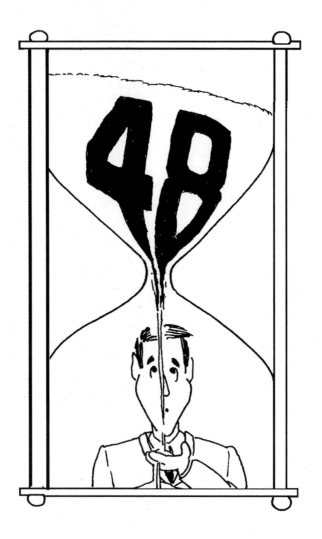

Robert now understands that planning, attitude and accountability are key ingredients to future success. Upon close introspection, Robert definitely felt "entitled" to that promotion that he was passed over for and unfortunately that attitude came out in the interview. Also, Robert now sees why his project team was replaced when they resorted to blaming rather than owning up to the missed deadline. Both situations seem so clear in retrospect. He is encouraged by these realizations and is ready to move onto the next career differentiator.

The next area that needs to be tackled is responsiveness. Robert tends to let things pile up and will miss critical deadlines as a result. He hates to let people down but sometimes he just can't get through the stack of "to do's" in a timely manner. To stand apart from the rest Robert needs to be proactive and efficient. Following one simple rule – the 48-hour rule – will bring the results that Robert desires.

→ The 48-Hour Rule

We can all agree that business today is traveling "faster than the speed of thought." Yet, have we taken the time to acknowledge the skills and approach needed to compete in today's fast-paced economy?

Whether you're trying to promote an idea, solve a problem, or push a project forward, the tempo at which you operate will surely influence your ultimate success. We no longer have the luxury of extended periods of time to capture a market or command someone's attention because in today's economy everything seems to move at high speed. Time is the very commodity that is at risk. We have more communication, more problems to solve and more opportunities than ever before. What are the new rules? How fast do we need to act? What failsafe methodology can we embrace to ensure that we are in the driver's seat, at least most of the time?

The 48-hour rule is one key to success. The 48-hour rule, simply stated, stipulates that to more effectively seize a new opportunity you should follow up or perform an action within 48 hours after interest has been established. Why? Because after 48 hours momentum is lost. Mind share is gone. New problems have arisen.

The 48-hour rule is easy to understand but difficult to implement. Most people use a similar clock speed for every situation. How many times have you left a meeting with a list of action items firmly planted in the forefront of your mind only to return to your computer to find thirty new e-mails requiring your immediate attention? The fresh ideas and actions from your meeting go into the vortex of "to do's" crowding your digital organizer only to be acted upon at a much later time. Your advantage is lost!

How can you make the 48-hour rule work for you? Follow these six simple steps and you will begin to adjust your clock speed. In doing so you will differentiate yourself from the pack and reap significant rewards.

Steps to implement the 48-hour rule:

The first step is to acknowledge or agree with the concept. If you've never considered the issue of timing as it relates to capturing a competitive advantage, then now is the time to accept that Internet speed is driving our world. We need new rules to help guide us through cyberspace. As Bill Gates said in his book *Business @ The Speed of Thought,* "If the 1980's were about quality and the 1990's were about reengineering, then the 2000's will be about velocity."

The second step is to analyze your current sense of urgency. How do you react to opportunities that arise with clients, colleagues or your boss? What is the typical *lag time* between an identified idea and action on your part? Have you noticed a difference between the times when you've acted right away versus the times when you've waited to respond?

Test the 48-hour rule. Pick a few important projects and take *immediate* action after meetings or after new ideas are introduced. Learn to prioritize those projects that are aligned to your goals. How does it feel? How do others respond? Do the results differ from times when you've waited three or four days (or more!) to act? Ask a couple of co-workers or your manager for feedback. Have they noticed a difference?

Commit to the 48-hour rule. It may be a subtle change from your current approach but as everyone knows, the difference between winners and losers can be as small as a nanosecond.

Share the concept with your employees, teammates and others with whom you work. Let them see you set the pace and how much is accomplished as a result. Create an environment of momentum, progress and speed.

Reap the rewards. Embracing the 48-hour rule will differentiate you with clients, colleagues and your boss. You will earn the reputation of a doer and someone who knows how to get to the end zone. In a world of lots of ideas but little ability to execute properly or expeditiously, you'll stand out.

It may take some effort to synchronize your approach over the long term. Start slowly and try one new concept at a time. As you gain efficiencies you will also gain time which will give you the momentum to continue. As Bob Davis, founder of LYCOS and author of *Speed is Life, Street Smart Lessons from the Front Lines of Business* points out,

> *"Speed saves lives in all fields, of course, but in business today it is the great differentiator, an essential survival tool. We live in a world where a company is measured by its ability to accelerate everything from manufacturing to marketing, from hiring to distributing. If we can produce or process something faster, we can often do it for less money, serve our customers better and get a jump on our competitors. For almost any business these days, speed is indeed life."*

Toolkit Tips:

- Analyze your current level of responsiveness.

- Apply the 48-hour rule.

- Share the 48-hour rule with co-workers.

! "Light travels through space at a constant 186,281 miles per second. The laws of the universe dictate this speed with no deviation. Humans travel through life without the benefit of a fixed velocity. We move at a variable rate that fluctuates according to our capacity for assimilating new information and influences."
Daryl R. Conner
Managing at the Speed of Change

Say What?

A sales person was discussing an issue with a client and uncovered a sizeable new business opportunity. The client was anxious to solve the problem and they both agreed that the sales person would prepare a proposal for consideration. The sales person left with a sense of urgency, assuring the client that he would get right to work on the proposal. Back at the office the sales person was distracted and put the proposal off for a few days to take care of some immediate issues that had come up. A week later the sales person called the client to set a meeting to review the proposal. The client apologized but said that they found another way to solve the problem. *Had the sales person applied the 48-hour rule, they would have more business today.*

A group met to plan the company picnic. They brainstormed lots of ideas and discussed the need to investigate some of the ideas further. The meeting was highly energized with enthusiasm for the upcoming picnic. They were in the middle of a great discussion about possible food and game options when another group came to claim the conference room. The picnic planners quickly decided to meet again in a couple of days. Unfortunately no one had taken notes or agreed to any actions. They spent the entire second meeting trying to remember all the good ideas from the first meeting. *If the group had agreed to actions before the meeting ended and applied the 48-hour rule they could have spent the second meeting finalizing the event.*

Big news! Robert has been asked to lead a high profile corporate initiative. The assignment is to evaluate and implement one of the aspects of the company's e-commerce plan. Robert will pick the team, map out the project scope and implement the strategy. Armed with a sense of urgency and his other new skills; Robert is ready for operation cooperation.

→ Operation Cooperation

It's mysterious. It's elusive. You know when you have it but don't quite know how to get it when you don't. I'm talking about the synergy and triumph that comes with a high performing team. The dream team. It's the group that exudes the confidence associated with winning and the experience that allows them to do it over and over again. The delicate mix of skills, experience, drive and personality traits that create a hand in glove fit to achieve superior results. Some of us have never had this kind of experience. Some of us have had it once and spend the rest of our career looking for it again. Some are lucky enough to replicate the magic over and over again. What are the components of a high performing team? How do you sustain cooperation over time? How will the teams of the future differ from those of the past?

Is it possible to avoid teamwork today? Doubtful. Whether it's a team of two or twenty, most of us need the cooperation of others to solve a problem or tackle a project. However, teams aren't always effective. Trying to blend personalities, diverse backgrounds and diverse outlooks can be disastrous. Dysfunctional teams can be found everywhere. Examples include:

- Teams without clear goals.
- Teams with in-fighting.
- Teams that lack accountability for progress.
- Teams with no leadership or too much leadership.
- Teams that are dominated by one person.
- Teams that succumb to political pressures.
- Teams without the skills, abilities or resources to accomplish the task.

Since teamwork is a tangible reality for most of us and the pitfalls associated with teamwork are plentiful, it may be prudent to delve into the attributes of successful teams. Let's take a look at what some experts say about teamwork and then take their advice to the streets.

Author and Coach Pat Riley, *The Winner Within*

"Excellence is never having learned enough. A few seasons in competitive sports teaches you how success can lull people. Teams who stay on top know different ... and they live it: **Excellence is the gradual result of always wanting to do better.**

You also gotta set the stage for people to excel. No attitude lecture can take the place of the environment that leaders create for their people. A sound, energized environment allows excellence to happen because a leader has to help talent want to do its best."

Author Patricia Fripp, *The Genius of Teamwork*

> *"True teamwork is the rarest, most exhilarating, and most productive human activity possible. Every business wants to harness this incredible energy but achieving such a level of motivation and esprit is not always easy. A team is not just a group of individuals who work at the same location or have the same logo on their business card."*

Futurist Bob Treadway CSP from Littleton, Colorado often gives the Mensa IQ Test to participants in his seminars. He has found that many "average" people, when working as a team, test at "genius" level or higher. Treadway finds that a team "becomes a genius when everyone works together."

Treadway also noticed that when a team is working at optimal performance, it is hard to know who the leader is. In other words, the team runs the team.

We can see some themes starting to emerge. Trust, clarity of purpose, respect for fellow team members and the development of a team spirit which is fostered by a strong leader are themes that resonate throughout the perspectives. We all know that teams go through various stages of development. The typical evolution stages include forming, storming, norming and performing. The trick is this: how do you accelerate a team's movement through these stages to achieve sustained excellence? **The Operation Cooperation Checklist** will help your team to build a solid foundation. Following the simple checkpoints will accelerate team growth and help the team concentrate on the task at hand rather than the mechanics of building a team. The checklist includes three phases of team development: Building a strong foundation, getting to work, and enjoying the journey. Most teams tend to get to work without building a strong foundation. These teams have a hard time reaching their goals or sustaining their success. Just as you might suspect, teams without a solid foundation will crumble during the slightest shake up. Team members as well as team leaders can use this checklist. As we learned from Bob Treadway, when a team is working at optimal performance, leadership comes from the team as a whole.

Let's put 'Operation Cooperation' to work. As David W. Johnson and Frank P. Johnson said in *Joining Together* "Every excellent group begins with a dream shared by most members. Group members become the keepers of the dream."

The Operation Cooperation Checklist

Phase One – Building a Strong Foundation:

- ❑ Find a team leader who is experienced, committed and talented at leading groups.

- ❑ Build your team with the strongest players available.

- ❑ Set a clear charter for the group. (Vision, mission, goals)

- ❑ Tie goals to incentives for achievement.

- ❑ Clearly delineate the scope of the project.

❑ Develop ground rules for group management.

❑ Set clear expectations for behaviors and results.

❑ Address issues about trust, respect, listening and valuing diversity up front.

❑ Team leaders must weed out dysfunctional behavior and hidden agendas and address them immediately.

❑ Incorporate team building activities into meetings to develop interpersonal relationships throughout the team.

❑ Create an environment where diverse ideas and creative thinking are accepted and encouraged.

❑ Make a list of each team members strengths and weaknesses. Find ways to build on the strengths of the group.

❑ Encourage cooperation rather than competition among group members.

Phase Two - Getting To Work:

❑ Discuss how the group will make decisions.

❑ Incorporate problem solving and planning skills into the group's process.

❑ Agree on vehicles for measuring the group's progress.

❑ Ensure that all meetings are productive by distributing an agenda in advance.

❑ Start meetings by reviewing the goals and progress towards the goals. Review action items from previous meeting.

❑ Ensure that all team members have a role in the meeting.

❑ End meetings with an assessment of what was effective and what should be changed for next time.

❑ Brainstorm on-going resources to help the group move forward.

❑ Identify stakeholders and keep them appraised of the group's progress.

❑ Document all action items including who will do what and when.

❑ Keep a sense of urgency to keep the project moving.

Phase Three – Enjoying the Journey:

- ❑ Create opportunities for team members to pursue their own best ideas.

- ❑ Draw in quiet members with open-ended questions.

- ❑ Share the team's progress and successes with all sponsors and stakeholders.

- ❑ Continually look for ways to bring new information to the team.

- ❑ Bring in experts to foster team growth.

- ❑ Encourage and acknowledge great ideas and creative thinking.

- ❑ Recognize individual team members for exceptional contributions.

- ❑ Reward team accomplishments.

The Operation Cooperation Checklist will ensure that your team covers all the bases necessary for group success. The final ingredients that must be added to create 'The Dream Team" are passion for the mission, an unrelenting determination to be successful and a complex mixture of experience, talent, cooperation and competitive drive. These components ensure high levels of performance that can be sustained over time.

How will teams of the future differ from those of the past? Clearly the need for teamwork will continue to accelerate.

The basic components of building a team will most likely remain unchanged. However, the challenges will become greater. New challenges will include:

- Cultural differences
- Language differences
- Logistical challenges such as time differences
- Varying communication platforms

To overcome the new challenges it will be increasingly critical to lay the proper foundation for teams to flourish. Isn't it about time for operation cooperation at your place of work?

 Toolkit Tips:

✏ Effective teams can be one of the most powerful tools to achieve superior results.

✏ Experts say that teams must start with a strong leader, have a clear purpose and embrace trust, respect and diversity.

✏ Follow the **Operation Cooperation Checklist** to build a strong foundation, produce great work and enjoy the journey.

! "Teamwork is the essence of life. If there's one thing on which I'm an authority, it's how to blend the talents and strengths of individuals into a force that becomes greater than the sum of its parts. My driving belief is this: great teamwork is the only way to reach our ultimate moments, to create the breakthroughs that define our careers, to fulfill our lives with a sense of lasting significance."
Pat Riley, *The Winner Within*

Say What?

A national team has one member that consistently withholds information and refuses to cooperate with the team. The team leader is intimidated by this team member and allows this dysfunctional behavior to continue much to the frustration of the rest of the team. *This team will have a hard time being successful. The team leader or a strong team member must address the issue so the team as a whole can move forward.*

A process improvement task force includes the President's assistant. Each time a decision is made the team yields to the assistant to assure that all decisions are consistent with the President's point of view. *This team is missing the opportunity for breakthrough thinking and decision making by succumbing to political pressures.*

Robert was enormously successful leading the project team on the e-commerce initiative. The team received company wide recognition for their efforts. Robert had a chance to incorporate almost all of the 'over the top' skills that were now so familiar to him. However, during the course of the project he noticed that personal interaction and communication were the glue that held all the components together. The team went through periods of "good" communication and periods of "bad" communication. Robert confided to his advisor that leading a complex team with a critical mission was not only pressure packed but also required a certain amount of finesse. The advisor pointed out that Robert's style of communication would set the tone for the groups progress and interactions. The advisor suggested that Robert look over, "He Said, She Said" for some quick do's and don'ts to help him avoid the common communication pitfalls in the future.

→ He Said, She Said

Communication is a vast topic. It underlies all our interactions and solid communication skills are essential to success in business. The information available on communication is widespread and ranges from a university degree to the plethora of books on the topic to unending Internet tidbits.

However, there are some basic do's and don'ts that will give us an immediate boost to our ability to interact and communicate effectively at work. They fit into the category of basic business tools of communication etiquette.

Do: Force yourself to truly listen to others.

Don't: Contemplate lunch alternatives or stock picks while co-workers are sharing important information.

Do: Be sensitive to gender insinuations.

Don't: Use "she" when referring to administrative tasks or jobs. (It's amazing how frequently this still happens.)

Do: Return phone calls in a timely manner (the 48-hour rule).

Don't: "Blow anyone off" at work, even a sales person, as they may be your co-worker or boss at some future point in time.

Do: Prepare for large and small "presentations". Defer if you're unsure about the answer to a question.

Don't: Think that people can't tell when you're "flying by the seat of your pants."

Do: Ask for help and give people a chance to assist.

Don't: Create a fire drill by asking two or more people to solve the same problem thereby wasting everyone's time.

Do: Pay attention during meetings.

Don't: Show up for a meeting late and ask questions about the material that was covered early in the agenda.

Do: Take a second to consider the right vehicle for communication. (e.g., in person, group meeting, phone, e-mail, voice mail, snail mail, etc.)

Don't: Deliver bad news on voice mail, call a meeting when an e-mail would suffice or use e-mail as a substitute for team building.

Do: Use the 24-hour rule (not to be confused with the 48-hour rule for follow up) and wait to respond when dealing with an emotionally charged situation.

Don't: React or lead with emotions as you'll probably say something that you'll regret later.

Do: Treat e-mail as semi-formal communication. Be deliberate with use of "Reply to all" and "Blind copy".

Don't: Forget to spell check all e-mails whether internal or external. Write in full sentences and use proper English. Don't assume your e-mail isn't a matter of public record and won't be used in court some day.

Do: Take the time to give honest, constructive feedback to co-workers.

Don't: Resort to blaming when the situation goes awry.

Do: Use professional language. Dress for success. (Use a personal shopper if you're not sure what this means.) Know your basic business manners. (e.g., how to introduce someone, handshake etiquette, etc.)

Don't: Forget that any face to face communication with someone begins **before** you start talking.

Do: Ask for someone's time before launching into a long discussion.

Don't: Ask if someone has a minute then proceed to take twenty minutes of his or her time.

Do: Engage in positive, constructive discussions.

Don't: Gossip or spread rumors.

Do: Share your professional values with the people that work with you or for you.

Don't: Act in ways that contradict your stated core values.

Do: Have someone proofread important documents like project plans, proposals, or memos.

Don't: Underestimate the power of the written word.

Robert took to heart the do's and don'ts. He realizes that communication and personal interactions can make or break a team's success. From his recent experience, he would add two essential aspects of communication to the list. The first is the criticality of setting clear expectations early on in a project. Expectations can take the form of ground rules for behavior, expectations for results or both. People feel more comfortable when everyone is working from the same rulebook. Expectations should also be a two-way street. If you're setting expectations, don't forget to ask what is expected in return. Clear expectations, mutual agreement and commitment will ensure the relationship starts on solid footing.

The second communication must is the necessity to give (and receive) on going feedback. Most people, including managers and leaders, lack the courage to offer constructive feedback. During the course of Robert's recent project, there were many times when a team member's actions contradicted the agreed upon ground rules. It took a lot of courage but Robert tried to address each situation to keep the team on track. However, as we will learn in the next chapter "Memo to the Masses" team members must also take the initiative to give appropriate feedback to co-workers. As Robert confided to his advisor previously, leading a team is highly rewarding but also puts your communication and personal interaction skills to the test.

Toolkit Tips:

✏ Communication and interpersonal skills are the 'glue' to cement all other professional traits.

✏ Be mindful of the basic do's and don'ts when interacting with others.

✏ Listening skills are far more important that talking skills.

❗ "The most basic of all human needs is the need to understand and be understood. The best way to understand people is to listen to them."

Ralph Nichols

Say What?

A senior manager gives recognition at a sales meeting and mispronounces *most* of the names of the people receiving the accolades.

An employee requests a meeting with his manager to discuss an important issue. The manager listens for several minutes, his eyes glaze over, and then he mindlessly starts checking e-mail. *This everyday occurrence demonstrates the lack of general listening skills that seem to be pervasive today.*

A Human Resources Director plays his daily voice mails on speakerphone with his door open for anyone in the general vicinity to hear their fellow employees most sensitive and confidential information.

In his book *7 Survival Skills for a Reengineered World*, William Yeomans lists nine reasons why people in work situations often don't listen:

1. Your mind does not like to pay attention.
2. You think faster than people talk.
3. People are boring.
4. You rehearse your responses while people are talking.
5. You have too much on your mind.
6. Listening puts you in a "second-class" role.
7. You think the speaker is a loser.
8. You don't believe much anyone tells you anyway.
9. You can't hear.

There are many trends in the workplace. Some involve dramatic changes and some are subtle shifts. One of the subtle shifts is the blurring of traditional roles, especially the roles of employee and manager. Robert discusses this trend with his advisor. Robert is especially interested in this area because he tends to shift roles at work depending on his assignment. Sometimes he's a manager, sometimes he's a project leader and sometimes he's a team member. The advisor commends Robert on his insight. He also points out how important it is to stay flexible with your perception of your role at work. Many careers are derailed by the intense rate of change causing restructuring, elimination of management and a ripple down effect touching almost every employee. Some people simply can't adjust quickly enough to keep up. He told Robert to continue to look for trends, listen to market signals, learn what they mean and respond accordingly. To underscore his point, the advisor shared the following memo to the masses.

➜ Memo to the Masses

Date: 2000's and beyond

To: All Employees

From: Senior Management

RE: Congratulations, all workers have been promoted to management

Effective immediately all employees are responsible for managing themselves. Formal training is under development and will be released at a later time. (However, due to market conditions, budget constraints and other immediate business priorities, we have re-directed the training staff to revenue generating activities. In other words, proceed without training.)

Each of you will be expected to understand and execute the business priorities, develop a plan (for yourself) to achieve the goals and give yourself feedback along the way. You should be adept at problem solving, process improvement and decision making. You are also responsible for your own career plan and career development. We are looking for an environment of total accountability and self-directed focus. No excuses.

Please channel any questions to the proper resource. (It's your job to find out who, what and where any and all resources are located.) We're counting on you to grow revenues, reduce expenses, find new markets and customers and improve quality.

Thank you.

The change is subtle yet significant. Today, managers are expected to stay current and produce results and employees are expected to take more responsibility for traditional management activities. The lines have clearly blurred.

Why the shift? The current environment values the people who do the work, not the people who manage the people who do the work. The market dynamics demand flat, efficient organizations with very little overhead. Therefore, all employees have to pitch in and actively participate in the work that's required to get the job done.

What are the new job descriptions? How will the work be shared? Won't there be role confusion? These questions and many others will be answered over the course of time. In the meantime, here are a few tips to prepare for a business world in which roles are dynamic and job descriptions are virtual.

Which category applies to you: the old way or the new way?

The old way: Vision, mission, goals are the responsibility of senior management. Sometimes they're clear; sometimes they're not. Either way, they're someone else's areas of concern.

The new way: Seek out and participate in the vision, mission, and goals. Take the time to understand how they apply to your job. If the goals are unclear, seek clarification.

The old way: Large problems reside with management. You might point out an issue but it's certainly not your place to take any action if the problem doesn't relate to your area of responsibility.

The new way: If you see issues, seek to find alternatives and solutions. Simply pointing out the problem won't help the organization to move forward. Make the extra effort to send e-mail detailing the problem and several possible solutions. If appropriate, offer to jump in and help. If your organization doesn't have a "suggestion box" of some sort, suggest that one be implemented. Take the lead to replace complaining with positive proactive thinking and problem solving.

The old way: Attend company sponsored training, but only if it's a requirement. After all, who has time for training anymore?

The new way: Take responsibility for learning. Don't wait for company sponsored training events. Determine what skills and new areas of learning (your quiver of tools) will be required to meet and exceed the goals. Initiate a search for resources to get the requisite experience. Also, maintain the mindset that company paid training is a privilege, not an entitlement.

The old way: Managers try to hold their people accountable.

The new way: Be accountable for your actions and results. Eliminate confusion, excuses or simply dropping the ball. Don't agree to actions or goals that you're not prepared to meet.

The old way: Challenging your manager or senior management is only tolerated to a certain point. Any attempts are definitely treading on thin ice.

The new way: Formal titles or power positions do not dissuade you from making a solid argument for issues you feel strongly about, even if you disagree with the President or CEO. **Note:** challenging the status quo should be based on a foundation of facts, professionalism and respect for others. Also, challenging your manager does not always equate to getting your way.

The old way: Management initiates change. Change is something that happens to you and is generally not fun or comfortable.

The new way: Stay open-minded. If people, programs and processes can be challenged, then be ready to have your ideas challenged back. Remain flexible to change in the work environment. Recognize that change is normal and concentrate on the possibilities. Think beyond yourself and your situation. Ask yourself if the initiative on the table is

good for your customers, employees and
the company. If the answer is yes to all,
but "no" for you personally, try to climb
on board anyway. Most changes settle and
truly talented people always end up in a good
position even if they've experienced a short-
term setback. Also, staying ahead of the
change curve will give you the ability to help
affect the outcome.

The old way: Managers are responsible for
their employee's behaviors, skills and results.

The new way: Managers don't have time to
give employees constant feedback. Have a
clear picture of your strengths and areas of
opportunity. Develop feedback mechanisms
on your own. Ask teammates or co-workers
how you can be more effective. Notice the
subtle body language and signals of the people
you work with. Do people cut you off when
you're speaking? Maybe you are too verbose
or repeat yourself constantly? Develop a plan
to enhance your strengths and address your
areas of concern.

The old way: Employees wait for direction
and communication from management.
Managers give all recognition for
accomplishments.

The new way: Take the lead. Don't wait for
a manager or the organization to recognize
superior efforts and results. Recognize
those you work with and celebrate big
accomplishments. Information and

communication should come from anyone and everyone, not just management. As Bill Gates says in his book *Business @ The Speed of Thought,* "A company's middle manager and line employees, not just its high-level executives, need to see business data. Companies should spend less time protecting financial data from employees and more time teaching them to analyze and act on it."

The old way: Employees have one manager. Managers ask for things that employees really don't want to provide, e.g., status reports, updates, forecasts or budgets projections.

The new way: Manage your manager. You may have multiple managers depending on the project or line of business. Identify all your managers. Manage these people (really your customers) by providing constant up-to-date information in all areas that may be of interest to them. Don't wait for them to ask you for information. Anticipate what they need and provide it in advance. Initiate discussions and make time for planning on important matters. Give them a periodic review of your performance. The idea is to free them up to help with the work at hand. Appreciate any efforts they put forth to make your day easier.

The list could go on but the point is that the focus has shifted from workers and managers with distinctly different roles to a virtual patchwork of skills and abilities needed to get the job done. People in all jobs and professions need to stay flexible and understand that from day to day they may be required to perform the role of project leader, sales person, technical support or president. Depending on the situation, you could be a manager or an employee, a customer or a supplier. The Internet is blind to these titles and an increasing amount of business is conducted each month without the need for traditional roles and layers of management. The trick is to enhance your ability to compete in this new environment.

 Toolkit Tips:

✏ The traditional distinction of roles between managers and employees has blurred.

✏ Embrace the new order. Start with clarity on organizational goals, take responsibility for learning, be accountable for your actions, and stay open-minded.

✏ Be proactive. Stay ahead of decisions that may affect your job by providing timely, relevant information to managers.

✏ Behave as if it's your own business. Act as if you have all the empowerment and resources at your disposal to solve problems and make changes to improve the environment around you.

Say What?

A front line employee is offended and discouraged when he interviews and doesn't get a management position. No one has the time or the courage to give this top performer the feedback that he has no management experience, a spotty personnel record and has never expressed any interest in management until this very moment. *The new way: Employees need to have an accurate picture of their skills and abilities. Employees should take the lead in making sure they have a development plan.*

A manager spends a week each month conducting forecasts and tracking down budget information. The manager is unavailable to help with key projects or answer questions during this time. *The new way: Employees should show initiative by anticipating the required information and provide that information in a pro-active manner. Managers should find a new way to approach those tasks that rob them of valuable time to participate in higher value activities.*

An employee has an excellent relationship with his manager. The relationship is based on trust and mutual respect. The manager is promoted and the new manager comes in with a totally different approach. All employees must re-prove themselves. The employee becomes frustrated with having to re-prove himself and lets his attitude slip. The new manger assesses this employee as capable but having a negative attitude. The relationship never improves. ***The new way:*** *Anticipate changes at work, especially in the management ranks. Take the time with new managers or co-workers to learn about their priorities. Share your approach and past successes and agree on the best way to work together productively.*

By this time, Robert and his advisor have spent hours and hours together. As a matter of fact, the advisor has really become a mentor. Robert is one of the fortunate few that have found a mentor who gives candid feedback, shares advice and helps promote him throughout his career. Personal promotion is something that Robert has done very little of. Robert is not one to talk about his personal accomplishments or significant successes. However, Robert is starting to realize that self-promotion is a fact of life. Recently he had the chance to do some lucrative freelance work but lost the opportunity to someone with an impressive portfolio. Robert has equally impressive work but can only speak to the content as he has never taken the time to organize his examples into a showcase. His mentor pointed out that, "It's not always comfortable to focus on selling yourself but neither is getting passed over for a premier assignment or losing your job. These are career realities today."

→ Myself, Inc.

When was the last time you thought about selling yourself? During your last job interview? Well, packaging yourself and understanding your key selling points may be more critical than ever.

According to Barbara Moses in her book *Career Intelligence – The 12 New Rules for Work and Life Success:*

> "People who work for large organizations now find themselves in the same position as consultants, freelancers and other independent contractors: endlessly gathering testimonials, documenting their achievements and making proposals for new pieces of work. Indeed, just like many consultants, they may find themselves spending as much time selling themselves for the work as actually doing the work. In today's workplace, workers have to constantly resell/market themselves - to

*constantly manage other people's
impressions of how well they are
performing."*

Why is promoting your abilities a new requirement? The
business environment has become a competitive, value
for value world. Simply doing a good job will not ensure
job success. The ability to sell your ideas and market
yourself is the key to thriving.

Whether you're a CEO, a departmental manager or just
trying to get ahead, the time is now to "shore up" your
ability to package "Myself, Inc."

Let's begin with some thought starters.

- ❑ Have you taken inventory of your strengths
  and weaknesses? What key benefits and value
  do you offer your company as well as the
  market? If you had to design a brochure
  to sell yourself, what would it say? What
  are you doing to differentiate yourself? Do
  you hire or surround yourself with people to
  compensate for your areas of weakness?

- ❑ Are you an end result thinker? What key
  accomplishments and skills will you add to
  your resume next year? Do you know what
  the emerging skills are in your field that will
  be necessary for success in the future?

- ❑ Do you exemplify professionalism? Do you
  always go the "extra mile" by sending thank
  you notes, key information or articles to
  business associates or clients? Are you ever
  alert to new ideas and suggestions which may
  help you in your career?

❑ Do you affiliate with people and organizations that are aligned to your career interests? Do you stay in touch with business associates, previous employers and professional friends? Are they aware of your accomplishments?

❑ Do you consistently promote yourself? Do you seek out opportunities for speaking engagements or publishing articles in your field? Do you keep an up-to-date personal portfolio with a current resume, biography and record of achievements?

❑ Do you have a mentor? Have you developed a trusted advisor who gives you candid feedback and ideas? Does your mentor act as an advocate for you?

❑ If you're a manager, do you help your employees with their professional development? Do you offer suggestions to help them promote themselves? Do you act as a champion for their best efforts?

❑ If you're part of a team, does the team share their approach with other teams? Does the team publicize successful results? Does the team celebrate their accomplishments?

Now that we are aware of some of the key areas of personal promotion, where do you start?

Try following the **Quick Start Promotion Guide**. These simple techniques will help enhance your ability to package yourself, but best of all you don't have to be an expert in sales or marketing to get results. As Barbara

Mosses points out in her book, *Career Intelligence – The 12 New Rules for Work and Life Success*:

> *"We have all had to sell ourselves at one time or another, whether in interviewing for a job, pitching a boss to get sent on a training course, or selling a piece of business to a client. What is new, though, is the need to sell ourselves hard, all the time."*

Quick Start Promotion Guide

Tip ❶

Create a Career Management file. It might be a file in your desk or on your computer desktop or both. This will give you one spot for all your career information.

Tip ❷

Re-cap your work accomplishments on a regular basis. Monthly may be too frequent for some but semi-annually should be the maximum duration. The re-cap should be directed to your manager and anyone else with a vested interest in your activities. Detail specific achievements, measurable results and significant contributions. Include all aspects of your work such as training, seminars, special projects and professional community involvement.

This is a simple, straightforward way to keep others up-to-date on your successes. It also helps you to be result-oriented. With companies selling off divisions and the rate of management turnover, you'll be amazed how useful this tool can be. An example of a work accomplishment re-cap document can be found at the end of this chapter.

Tip ❸

Ask for letters of recommendation that describe your successes. Letters can come from clients, co-workers, vendors, managers or professional volunteer organizations. Request a letter immediately. If you wait until you need these letters (e.g., when interviewing for a job), it's too late. People change positions, leave companies or accomplishments become a vague memory. Note: you may have to offer to draft this letter yourself or provide some samples to follow. These letters can be difficult to write and your request may slip to the bottom of his/her priority list.

Tip ❹

Give the Human Resources Department (as well as your manager) a copy of all awards, letters of recognition or recommendation, training certifications and work accomplishment reports. Ask them to place these in your personnel file. Virtually every company keeps personnel files and it's up to you to manage what's found in your file.

A good hiring manager or new manager will review employees personnel files to get background information, so this is yet another opportunity to make a good impression.

Tip ❺

Create a career portfolio. Invest in a nice leather binder and clear plastic sheet protectors. Gather all your career accomplishments and place them in the binder. This becomes the "evidence" of your accomplishments. (It also makes you feel better during tough times to page through your portfolio.) Your portfolio should include original letters of recommendation, awards, training certificates, certifications and samples of showcase work.

All of these things can be found in your Career Management file. Include extra plastic sleeves in your binder so it's easy to stay current. A career portfolio can be used during a job interview, with a new client or as a tool to secure freelance business.

Tip ❻

Keep a career summary. Catalog each position, dates, key accomplishments, training and skill development. This document will serve as a source log that can be easily used to create a resume, biography

or other career tool. It's too easy to forget
the details associated with various positions
as time goes on. This historical record can be
updated annually or during a job change. An
example of a career summary can be found at
the end of this chapter.

Tip ❼

Think beyond your resume. A resume is
simply a record of the past. A new employer
or client is more interested in what they can
expect from you in the future. How will
your skills and abilities benefit the team and
help the organization move forward? Think
of yourself as a consultant. How would you
design your brochure? Be creative. Use
color. Clearly this approach will differentiate
you from the crowd. As Gordon Miller,
author of **The Career Coach, Winning
Strategies for Getting Ahead in Today's Job
Market** points out,

*"But don't be mislead into thinking that just
because the balance of power has shifted,
you're automatically going to get that terrific
job or that big raise or that promotion
or stock option. Even though there's a
shortage of workers out there, there's still a
highly competitive environment for the top
positions. One of the reasons for this is
that employees are changing jobs a lot more
often than they did, moving from company to
company – job jumping – in search of new
and better opportunities. The way to put
yourself in the best possible light, no matter*

what your situation at your current job, is to market yourself as brand **You***."*

Try replacing or augmenting your resume with a brochure to sell yourself. Think of yourself as a company. Determine your target market. (e.g., job class or industry) What problems exist that you can solve? What are the opportunities that you can capitalize on? Detail your product or service. (e.g., your expertise, training, skills and abilities) What benefits do you offer? How are you different from others with a similar background? (e.g., track record, proven results) This project can be a difficult assignment and particularly nettlesome for those without a sales or marketing background, however, the concept is valuable.

An example of a personal brochure can be found at the end of this chapter.

Tip ❽

Find a mentor. Some people naturally fall into these relationships but for most of us we have to make a deliberate attempt to find an advisor. If you don't have a coach and don't know where to begin, start at the beginning with your career plan. Did you identify people who could help with your career goals? Maybe one of them could be a trusted advisor. The person should be ahead of you in their career and have a successful track record.

Find someone whom you respect. It's also helpful to find someone that is aligned to your basic values. A true mentor is a confidant during good times and bad and it's important to be comfortable with them under various circumstances. A mentor will give you candid feedback, encouragement and help promote you when you need a boost. Some people are lucky enough to have multiple mentors.

If you've identified someone but don't know him or her well, take the initiative to invite them to coffee or out to lunch. Prepare basic career advice questions and listen carefully to their answers. If you don't hit it off, move on. The relationship should be natural, light and fun. For those who have attained significant career success, are you mentoring others? If not, think about the difference you could make for someone else.

Tip ❾

Network. Now that you have all the career promotion fundamentals in place, it's time to expand your circle of friends. Find ways to meet new people aligned to your vocational interests. Join a professional association, take a class or join a networking group. Conduct informational interviews inside and outside of your organization on a regular basis. Volunteer boards are a great way to meet key business leaders and give to the community.

You may have noticed that many of the tips build on one another. The three fundamental tips are: the Career Management file, the Career Summary document and regular re-caps on your accomplishments. All other career building tools can be developed from these three sources. Start with the basics and grow your career arsenal over time.

As expert Peter Drucker says, "The best way to predict the future is to plan it."

One last critical point: Your personal PR plan works best on the foundation of a proven track record and the ability to achieve results in your industry. If you're not as strong as you'd like to be, begin now. Also, although selling yourself may sound self-serving, as you enhance your personal reputation, you also further the reputation of your company. Strike the balance between a humble demeanor and appropriate personal promotion. Becoming a career activist is not a luxury. It's the key to your future career success.

 **Toolkit Tips:**

✏ Each of us must get comfortable with marketing ourselves.

✏ Determine what areas need to be "shored up" in your personal PR efforts.

✏ Follow the **Quick Start Promotion Guide** to accelerate your progress.

! "But if we put the "big rocks" in first,
we reverse that tendency. (The tendency to
fill your time with crises, pressing problems
and deadlines.) We create a framework to
accomplish what we feel is important, around
which we can then "fit in" other activities."

Stephen R. Covey
First Things First

Say What?

A qualified candidate is applying for a top-
notch manager's job. He interviews well but
his resume has a misspelling of the company's
name. *Clearly, he didn't get the job.*

A senior executive loses his job after fifteen
years with the company. He is distressed
and can't figure out why it takes months
to prepare to find a new position. *This
executive was not prepared for the career
realities today. He thought he was exempt
from cutbacks because of his executive
status. Additionally, he spent all of his time
inwardly focused and neglected to build
a strong network or maintain a career
portfolio. When the time came for him to
market himself, he had to start from scratch.*

Accomplishments Re-cap sample

Memorandum

TO: Susan Harper
    I.T. Director

FROM: Robert C. James
      I.T. Manager

DATE: July 1

SUBJECT: Mid Year Results

January through June Financial Results:

- Saved the company over $138,000.00 through successful vendor negotiations on database software.

- Re-organized the help desk group eliminating two FTE's.

- Ahead of current year budget projections.

January through June Process Improvements:

- Developed and implemented I.T.'s first end user survey.

> *"Thank you for asking our opinion. It shows that the I.T. group is interested in our feedback and wants to improve current levels of service. My hat goes off to you for taking the first step."*
>
> *Kristi Ericson, Office Services Manager*

- Initiated an on-line tracking system for help desk work orders saving one man-day per week.

January through June Employee Satisfaction:

- Worked with the Human Resources Department to develop an employee satisfaction survey to be implemented in the fall.

- Created a contest to improve response times. Results were tracked and winners were announced at a team lunch celebrating our overall improvement in this area.

  > *"Robert, you're doing a great job keeping our group on track and motivated to improve response times. Thanks for the fun lunch. It was a real team building event."*
  > *Larry Jochim, Help desk*

January through June Training:

- Leadership Development training course completion.

- Level III Customer Service training completion.

- Published article in Computing Times about trends in I.T. support

Career Summary Sample

Robert C. James, May Update

Position	Dates
Technical Operations Manager Intelligence Systems, Inc.. Santa Clara, CA	May '97 - Present

Key Accomplishments

- Streamlined processes
  - Help desk
  - Network support
  - Server management

- Developed and implemented a comprehensive customer support process including key metrics to measure progress. Documented all processes for training.

- Gained efficiencies from consolidating and re-routing telecommunications.

- Reduced overall expenses on a monthly basis by 23%.

- Reduced employee turnover by 9% from May '99.

- Developed an I.T. customer service module for the new hire training. Deliver training each month.

- Joined the Information Technology Managers Council.

Training / Skill Development

- Competed I.S. Management Training

- Participate in Leadership Development training program.

- On-going Financial training from Chief Financial Officer.

- Completed I.S. Customer Service Training (Level III)

- Completed Internal Controls training

- Published article in Computing Times about trends in I.T. support

Robert C. James, May Update

Position	Dates
Help Desk Manager AP Computers, Inc. Pleasanton, CA	June '91 - May '97

Key Accomplishments

- Created and implemented a software version update system that resulted in $210,000 of savings for FY '95 through '98.

- Created a development plan for Help Desk employees. Provided a positive work environment coupled with candid feedback to allow for growth.

- Increased employee retention by 18% from FY '95 to FY '98.

- Negotiated several software vendor contracts, which resulted in a cost saving to AP Computers of over $160,000.

- Joined the Software Management Association. (Became Vice Chair of recruiting)

Training / Skill Development

- New Software certification

- Negotiating Skills Seminar

- Help Desk Tools for Today's Managers training

- Advanced Computing training

Robert C. James, May Update

Position	Dates
I.T. Specialist Argus Systems, Inc. Seattle, WA	Oct. '83 - June '91
California Polytechnic State University San Luis Obispo, CA	'78 to '82

Key Accomplishments

- Invited to participate on the new technology team. Made customer response time targets each year.

- Assisted with company wide software conversion process.

- Designed and maintained a customer database.

- Developed customized reporting for management.

- Graduated with a BS degree in Engineering.

- Graduated with Honors. Volunteer jobs included work at The Computer Center on campus.

- Internship at small software company.

- Self-funded college education.

Training / Skill Development

- Certified in basic software

- Customer Service Training

Myself, Inc. Brochure Sample

Business Issues and Opportunities:

☞ Do you have problems with I.T. support?

☞ Could your Help Desk use a little assistance?

☞ Are software version updates an impossible task?

☞ Are your response times running out of control?

If you answered "yes" to any of these questions, I can help.

Product:

Robert C. James
1447 Oak Street
Santa Clara, CA 95054
408-867-4397

Services Offered:

- Experienced I.T. and Help Desk management

- Excellent track record in response time control and other key metrics

- Proven processes to track version updates as well as the many other components of I.T. support

Product Specifications:

- B.S. in Engineering,
  California Polytechnic State University
- Ten years experience with I.T. support at
  Intelligence Systems, Inc.
- Five years experience
  in the computing environment at AP Computers, Inc.

Key Benefits:

- Your organization will benefit from someone skilled in
  I.T./Help Desk management.

- Your organization can expect a team player with
  seasoned technical and management expertise and
  extensive problem solving abilities.

- You can expect an immediate positive impact to
  your I.T. organization based on my well rounded
  background. Formal training courses include: Help
  desk Tools for Today's Managers, Advanced Computing
  and Management Metrics.

Product and Services Guarantee:

For a full disclosure on past accomplishments, please
contact:

Susan Harper	Brad Nortel
I.T. Director,	Systems Manager,
Intelligence Systems, Inc.	AP Computers, Inc.
408-867-5043	510-453-6170
Sharper@IS.com	Brad.Nortel@APcomputers.com

Robert C. James,

your single source for I.T. and Help Desk Management

Robert has come a long way and the satisfaction associated with his accomplishments and skill building are real confidence boosters. Also, somewhere along the way his advisor became a mentor. Now Robert's mentor introduces him to others who have achieved great things in their careers. The stories are inspirational and confirm that the focus placed on learning, a humble attitude and hard work will pay off in the long run. The mentor advises Robert to continue to pursue others who have been there and are willing to share their pearls of wisdom. In this way, Robert can continue to develop his winning edge.

→The Winning Edge

You're on the top of your game. Success consistently comes your way. You're making your own good luck and it feels great.

If you can relate to these statements then you're one of the lucky ones who has been able to maintain their "winning edge" over time. What do I mean by a "winning edge?" How do you maintain it? What happens if you lose it? We'll explore these questions and learn from some successful professionals about how they've sustained their winning edge over the long haul.

Webster's definition of "edge" includes advantage, upper hand, and head start. When I consider people who possess that certain "edge" I think about these characteristics: hard work, focus, intensity, consistency, talent and unwavering drive. These folks are also competitors; they're in the game to win.

Now some people may think that this topic is a bit dated. There was a lot of media attention about "winning" in the eighties and early nineties. In the book, *The Winner*

Within by Pat Riley, the renowned professional basketball coach describes the complexity of winning this way:

> *"All of those contacts and experiences have proved to me, over and over again, that the complex inner rhythms of teamwork – flows of ambition, power, cooperation, and emotion – are the keys to making dreams come true."*

During the 1990's no one had time to think about winning – there were simply too many opportunities to pursue and too much money to be made. But, as most of us know, the business world rarely generates any new ideas, just a repackaging and resurgence of timeless concepts. So now in the 2000's, when most organizations are in the process of trying to reinvent themselves, it is prudent to again consider what it takes to maintain a winning edge.

In a quest to shed some light on this topic I've asked a diverse, yet extraordinarily accomplished group of professionals some deceptively simple questions:

- How do you maintain your career edge?

- Has there ever been a period of time when you felt like you lost your edge?

- If so, what did you do to regain it?

In the course of our interviews we'll meet executives, consultants, athletes and a TOPGUN pilot. Each offers a unique perspective on his or her journey.

Maintaining Your Career Edge — Perspectives

Barb Pellow is the Gannett Chair for Integrated Publishing Sciences at the Rochester Institute of Technology. Barb has also held senior executive positions with IKON Office Solutions, CAP Ventures, Xerox Corporation and IBM.

> *"I truly have never focused on a career. I have always had the opportunity to have a job that I love and the luxury of working with very smart people. Because I have been so excited about the job content, I worked hard at what I was doing. A blend of hard work, a love of what you do, and a great team of people are the most critical success factors in any career. You need to have a passion for the job and share that same passion with others in the organization as well as the customers who buy your product or service. The key to maintaining a career path is continuous learning and growth."*

William Seidel Jr., US Navy Fighter Pilot. Bill flew F-14 Tomcats aboard the aircraft carrier USS CARL VINSON and also had a tour as an Adversary Pilot flying A-4 Skyhawks. Bill is now a Captain for American Airlines.

> *"To be recognized as a person who holds an edge above the rest takes many years of growth and maturity as a pilot. In the air we constantly compete against ourselves.*

Typically, we would do a 1v1; this is one pilot versus another. When flying similar airplanes, the only difference is the driver. It's a sterile and equal arena."

So what decides who wins and who loses?

"Aggressiveness, technical knowledge, maneuvering skills, confidence, patience, gamesmanship, anticipation, foresight, energy management, and the courage to experiment – these are the deciding factors. If each pilot played these virtues to the best, it could still be countered with any other virtue. Patience can be wiser than aggressiveness. The ability to read your opponents game plan and counter with the right moves is the name of the game. Are you reacting, mirroring or dictating the fight? Sounds like chess but add 6 g's and 800kts of closure.

Let's say you've done well today. A smart adversary will come back after learning your talents and you can be assured the next flight won't be the same. Be ready to experiment. Don't prioritize to win, but rather to gain a little more wisdom and confidence. Over the years I've gone from losing frequently, to winning occasionally, to winning most always.

So, how did I keep the edge? I figured if I was consistent, humble and willing to learn, time and experience would put me in the top ranks."

Jay Tyler, CEO of eBest Inc., an enterprise software company in Silicon Valley. Jay has also held senior positions with Clarify, The Gartner Group and Xerox Corporation.

> *"I guess my claim to fame is the ability to take feedback, good and bad and use it to my advantage. I use my two ears to listen and try to find the "gold" in everyone. Never lose hope or optimism, be humble but confident. Never forget your upbringing. Remember not to blink when things get really bad. Don't let your employees (clients, co-workers) know when you have a hockey game going on in your stomach. My real challenge in life is to be a good person and a good father."*

Kenneth M. Mirch II is a financial services executive and former NCAA 50 meter breaststroke champion.

> *"I think the most important element in maintaining your edge is consistent energy toward long-term goals. I try not to get too excited or upset about short-term events. This is easier said than done. I look at tough periods of time as opportunities to reinvent my business and myself. Good times and bad times never last forever. Maintaining a moderate attitude through the extremes is the key to consistent performance in both athletics and business."*

Regaining Your Edge — Perspectives

Dorinda Parker is Vice President of Business Development with M Squared Consulting Inc. out of San Francisco, CA . Dorinda has also held senior leadership positions with IKON Office Solutions and Xerox Corporation.

> *"Losing your edge is usually unexpected. It's that uneasy feeling that things are not on track, evidenced by lack of focus, low energy levels and a general malaise. For me, the loss of edge has been triggered by slow business, re-evaluation of direction or a turn of events caused by significant loss or change. To the contrary, if I am in the 'zone' no matter how complex or difficult the situation, the problem can be solved!"*

How do you re-group when you fall off-track or the challenge is stale?

> *"I have found I must get to work by re-creating a sharp focus. The competitive edge must be re-kindled on a new level. The habit of honing and maintaining your attitude is really what has been lost. The following are some strategies that have worked for me.*
>
> *Adopt a fresh perspective. Envision the early days in the job when you were just starting out, the time when everything was open to possibility and every challenge was an opportunity.*

*Accept responsibility for change and commit
to action (enthusiasm and creativity are
born of commitment).*

*Jump-start and stick with forming the habits
that result in positive action (e.g. exercise,
sports, reading, classes)*

*Connect with positive people and become
a student of success stories and winning
ventures.*

*Get together with other people who have
been there and know 'the way back.'*

*Your winning attitude will be regained
through finding a personal connection,
commitment and hard work. Let the work
begin and remind yourself that it is easier to
keep your edge honed than to restore it when
it is lost."*

**Tom Kinsman is the founder of Take AIM (Take
Action In Management), a management consulting firm
specializing in helping business people form positive
habits in management.**

*"In 1981 I was told that I would never walk
again. At that point I had been in pain for
over nine years and gone through multiple
back operations. When the doctor gave me
his final diagnosis, I knew I would prove*

him wrong. That same drive that has me walking, running and exercising today is what helped me regain my health and my edge.

There are three things I'd like to share about rebuilding your life or your career. The first is how important it is to go back to your core values when things get bad. You have to have a sense of purpose and conviction in your work. By re-focusing on your core, you're natural confidence will come back. In my case, my competitive nature and the on-going, lifelong voice that screams that I have something to prove constantly fuel the climb.

The second lesson I learned was during an extended stay at a pain clinic. The process of learning to deal with chronic pain was a life changing experience. The experience strengthened my inner core and left me with a renewed perspective, acceptance, stronger values and an overall calmness to forge forward. Today, the back pain is gone and my energies are directed towards positive career and personal endeavors.

The last key to regaining and maintaining career momentum is to have one or more mentors. In my practice I try to teach skills and inspire traits. Three long ago mentors, my grandparents and my best friend's father gave me insight, guidance, and the confidence to succeed."

Lessons Learned

Each of these achievers has his or her own story, yet we can find several threads of consistency in their messages. We know that maintaining your advantage takes years of hard work and the willingness to learn. The hard work part is pretty straightforward, but a commitment to continuous learning is also hard work. When was the last time you took a class or read an entire book relating to your profession? We also have found that these top performers seem to strike a balance between confidence and a humble demeanor that allows them to listen, learn and maintain the respect of others. As our TOPGUN Pilot points out, the goal is not to win but to gain more wisdom and confidence with each experience.

Regaining your advantage can be more challenging, however, several messages resonated throughout that were powerful lessons for us all. In each case a strong commitment to change is the key to turning the tide. As Coach Riley points out,

> *"To energize a team to break through to its goal, some message must ignite that energy. But the positive and courageous voice will always emerge, somewhere, sometime, for all of us. Listen for it, and your breakthrough will come."*

We determined that re-focusing on our core values or those habits that made us successful in the first place will help us set clear goals to re-gain our momentum. We were also reminded that a mentor or those who have been down a similar path are vital resources during difficult times.

It turns out that Webster's definition of "edge" is pretty accurate. If we want an advantage, upper hand or head start in our career there are no short cuts. Careers are hard work whether you're "winning" or not. Why not follow the path of our TOPGUN Pilot who over the years has gone from losing frequently, to winning occasionally, to winning most always.

 Toolkit Tips:

☞ Maintaining a winning edge takes hard work and a willingness and commitment to lifelong learning.

☞ Regaining your momentum is about re-focusing on core values and those habits that made you successful in the first place.

☞ There are times when you're building your winning edge, times when you're maintaining your edge, and times when you simply want to strike a balance.

→ Conclusion —
The Road Ahead

You're probably wondering what happens to Robert. It would be easy to report that Robert goes on to a flawlessly successful career, however, perfect careers are rare in the business world. Robert goes through the normal ups and downs associated with the super high-speed roller coaster ride that we're all on.

But Robert is successful. He now has the tools to manage even the most terrible turns. He uses the 48-hour rule on a daily basis. He approaches projects with an air of cooperation and accountability. Gratitude is definitely part of his attitude. He's diligent to his career plan and personal promotion, and while it is still a little foreign, it is now part of his on-going mindset.

Has Robert reached the 'career end zone'? Definitely not. Careers are a perpetual work in progress. Although it is important to celebrate accomplishments and reaching key pinnacles, the work is never done. The process of evaluation, feedback and growth is on going and requires a long-term commitment, persistence and discipline.

Robert's network of professional friends are a source of inspiration and his mentor continues to provide feedback, support and encouragement. Also, one of Robert's previous employees has asked him for some career help. Robert has graduated to the ranks of people that approach their professions with confidence, optimism and an expectation of winning. It has taken a lot of hard work but Robert has created a career advantage.

 **Toolkit Tips Summary:**

☞ Taking inventory of your skills and abilities is paramount to gaining insight before moving forward.

☞ It's important to get feedback from more than one source to paint a clear picture of your current skill assets and liabilities.

☞ Sometimes the most obvious career success skills such as speed, accountability and career planning are the most overlooked.

☞ Planning is as fundamental as hard work or basic job knowledge.

☞ The hardest part of the planning process is getting started and making a habit of staying with your plan.

- ✏ Practice your planning steps until they become second nature and can be used each day.

- ✏ Put your plan in writing. Make sure it's measurable. Keep it accessible. Review your plan frequently.

- ✏ Plan your career or your career may not turn out as planned.

- ✏ Put some gratitude in your attitude.

- ✏ Attitude is the ultimate form of differentiation.

- ✏ Practice showing appreciation each day and watch the positive impact that it will have on you and others.

- ✏ Are you a Role Model, Juggler, Opportunist, Flake, Lone Wolf or Finger Pointer at work?

- ✏ Have you considered the components of accountability: The understanding factor, the belief factor, the ability factor and the follow through factor?

- ✏ Don't underestimate the power of accountability, it is a subtle yet highly valued virtue in the business world.

✆ Analyze your current level of responsiveness.

✆ Learn to prioritize those projects and actions that are aligned to your goals.

✆ Apply the 48-hour rule.

✆ Share the 48-hour rule with co-workers.

✆ Effective teams can be one of the most powerful tools to achieve superior results.

✆ Experts say that teams must start with a strong leader, have a clear purpose and embrace trust, respect and diversity.

✆ Follow the **Operation Cooperation Checklist** to build a strong foundation, produce great work and enjoy the journey.

✆ Communication and interpersonal skills are the 'glue' to cement all other professional traits.

✆ Be mindful of the basic do's and don'ts when interacting with others.

✆ Listening skills are far more important that talking skills.

➥ The traditional distinction of roles between managers and employees has blurred.

➥ Embrace the new order. Start with clarity on organizational goals, take responsibility for learning, be accountable for your actions, and stay open-minded.

➥ Be proactive. Stay ahead of decisions that may affect your job by providing timely, relevant information to managers.

➥ Behave as if it's your own business. Act as if you have all the empowerment and resources at your disposal to solve problems and make changes to improve the environment around you.

➥ Each of us must get comfortable with marketing ourselves.

➥ Determine what areas need to be "shored up" in your personal PR efforts?

➥ Follow the **Quick Start Promotion Guide** to accelerate your progress.

➥ Maintaining a winning edge takes hard work and a willingness and commitment to lifelong learning.

✏ Regaining your momentum is about re-focusing on core values and those habits that made you successful in the first place.

✏ There are times when you're building your winning edge, times when you're maintaining your edge, and times when you simply want to strike a balance.

Say What?

Now, we all know that no one is perfect. I was reminded of this recently when I went to the gas station. I pulled up and asked the attendant, "Fill it up please." The attendant said, "Sure" but added, "Hasn't anyone told you that it's bad manners to speak with your mouth full?" Totally embarrassed, I mumbled a yes and thank you, put away the celery sticks I'd been munching and tried to avoid eye contact for the duration of my visit. Driving away (as quickly as possible) I marveled at how feedback can come in many forms and sometimes from unlikely sources. The trick is to hear the voice, listen to the message and incorporate the lesson.

Sample Forms

Professional Effectiveness Scale

Tally Sheet

Name:

Date:

'Over the top' Differentiators	Score	Possible Gap	Priority
Planning			
Attitude			
Accountability			
Speed			
Cooperation			
Communication			
Career Management			
Total			

Goal Card Sample

Goals: Timeframes:

Strategies to achieve Goals:

1.

2.

3.

Training or experience required for goal achievement:

People that can help me achieve my goals:

Obstacles to overcome:

What will happen after I achieve my goals (Celebration):

Career Action Plan Sample

Short Term Career Goals: (1-2 years)

Long Term Career Goals: (3-5 years)

Areas of Strength:

Opportunities Areas:

Next 12 Month Focus	Action Step	Resources Needed	Date

Note: Action steps should include a combination of building on current strengths and focusing on areas for development.

Accountability Counts

Project:

Date of Meeting:

Date of Next Meeting:

Action Item	Person Responsible	Targeted Completion Date	Actual Completion Date	Comments

Accomplishments Re-cap sample

Memorandum

TO:

FROM:

DATE:

SUBJECT:

Financial Results:

Process Improvements:

Projects Completed:

Employee Satisfaction:

Training/Professional Development:

Career Summary Sample

Position	Dates	Key Accomplishments	Training / Skill Development

Myself, Inc. Brochure Sample

Business Issues and Opportunities:

Product:

Services Offered:

Product Specifications:

Key Benefits:

Product and Services Guarantee:

About the Author

Lisa D. Magnuson has years of experience as a sales, management and team building strategist. She has put these principles into practice throughout her career while working at Fortune 500 companies, Xerox Corporation and IKON Office Solutions. She has held executive roles on higher education boards and has published articles on topics ranging from business etiquette to building a top notch sales force. Lisa has been recognized nationally for her skills in business leadership, employee satisfaction and sales results. Born and raised in Menlo Park, California, Lisa now resides with her family in Portland, Oregon.

For more information visit

www.the48hourrule.com
or
www.toplinesales.com

More Books from MC2

Designing a Document Strategy
by Kevin Craine

This book targets managers, technicians and consultants who see the benefit and cost savings inherent in implementing a document strategy. The 5-phase process is tailorable to any environment, and includes Cause-effect diagrams, flow charts, and ROI formulas to copy and use. Case examples apply the theories in the real world, leading to meaningful and informed action. With this book as a guide, readers will be more likely to bring about real-world, bottom-line benefits. There is no better educational resource on designing a document strategy than this book.

Only $29.95
plus shipping

Wrestling Legacy Data to the Web & Beyond: Practical Solutions for Managers & Technicians
by P.C. McGrew & W.D. McDaniel

Here's the book for everyone in the document chain, including managers, designers, strategists and print programmers. *Wrestling Legacy Data* gives you the background on line data, AFP and Metacode/DJDE print formats as well as PostScript, PCL and PDF. Learn the resource terms that will help you communicate effectively with your vendors, plus tips on resolving common problems, There is also an appendix of vendors from around the world who can help!

Only $29.95
plus shipping

Critical Mass: A Primer for Living with the Future
by Pat McGrew & Bill McDaniel

Are you facing the technology squeeze? Adopt too early and the executives question your sanity. Adopt too late and you're called a dinosaur. This quick-to-read primer can help you make better decisions on the road to the future. There is no better resource for anyone who feels overwhelmed by the rapid pace of change and needs to find a baseline to understand how we evolved to where we are today.

Only $15.00
plus shipping